I can draw people

Ray Gibson

Illustrated by Amanda Barlow

Edited by Fiona Watt

Series editor : Jenny Tyler

I can draw...

a workman

1. Use a crayon to draw a hard hat.

2. Add a face, nose and hair.

3. Crayon a T-shirt.

4. Crayon a pair of blue jeans.

5. Add arms, hands and big boots. Fill in with felt-tip pens.

Draw things you would see on a building site, such as bricks and tools.

3

an angel

1. Draw a head with a fat felt-tip pen.

2. Crayon the face and some hair.

3. Draw a dress.

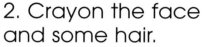

4. Add some sleeves.

5. Draw some hands and feet.

6. Add wings and a halo. Use crayons to fill in the angel.

a giant

1. Use a felt-tip pen to draw a head. Add some hair.

2. Add the body and his eyes, nose and mouth.

3. Add a beard. Draw the arms and his hands.

4. Add a belt below his body, then draw his legs.

Add tiny people, trees and animals to show how big the giant is.

Draw his castle on a hill in the distance.

5. Draw big
boots and
add a jacket,
like this.

6. Fill in the
giant and his
clothes with
crayons.

a pirate

1. Draw the head with a crayon. Add a head scarf.

2. Draw a face. Add a black eyepatch.

3. Draw an earring and a black beard.

4. Add the body. Draw circles for the hands.

5. Draw the arms. Join them onto the hands.

6. Add short legs and a pair of big black boots.

7. Draw one or two belts and a short jacket.

8. Fill the pirate in with different felt-tips.

Draw a hot sun and a palm tree.

Draw a boat in the sea.

Draw a treasure chest and some jewels.

a queen

1. Use a pen to draw a crown and a head.

2. Add the top part of her dress.

3. Add a big skirt and puffy sleeves.

4. Draw the arms and hands.

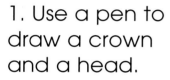

5. Add her hair, face and shoes.

6. Fill her in with crayons.

Add some jewels.

Add some patterns to her skirt.

Draw a king. Give him a beard.

a ballerina

1. Use a crayon to draw a head.

2. Draw her hair and face.

3. Draw the top part of her dress.

4. Do the
sleeves and
the skirt.

5. Add her
arms, hands
and legs.

6. Add some
shoes. Fill her
in with pens.

a soccer player

 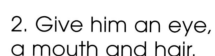

1. Draw a head and a nose with a pen.

2. Give him an eye, a mouth and hair.

3. Draw a shirt and the top of his arms.

4. Add some shorts and the top part of his legs.

5. Add the rest of his arms, hands and legs.

6. Give him socks and soccer boots. Fill in with crayons.

Draw the crowd.

Add a goal
keeper and a ball.

Add stripes
or patterns to
the shirt.

15

a scuba diver

1. Use a felt-tip to draw a head. Add a hood.

2. Add a nose, mouth and goggles.

3. Draw the body with a felt-tip.

4. Add the arms, hands and legs.

Draw some fish, a shark and an octopus.

5. Draw a flipper on each leg.

6. Draw an air tank on the back.

7. Add an air pipe and a mouthpiece.

8. Fill in with different crayons.

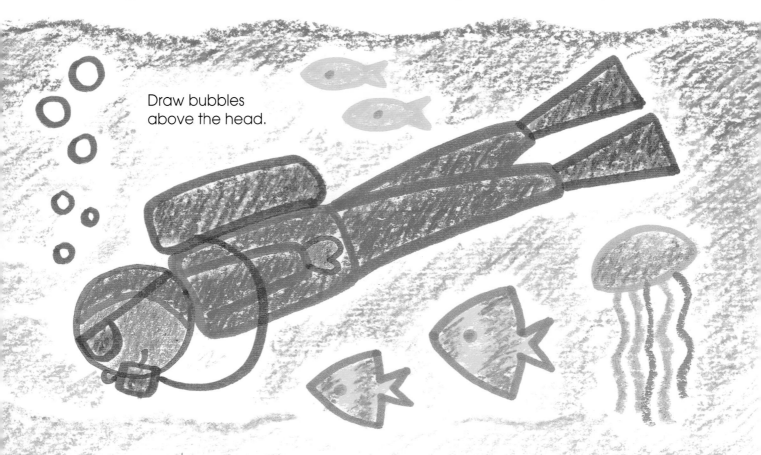

Draw bubbles above the head.

an astronaut

1. Draw the helmet with a felt-tip.

2. Draw two lines for a collar. Add a visor in the helmet.

3. Draw the astronaut's face inside the visor.

4. Use a felt-tip to add the body of the spacesuit.

5. Draw fat arms and legs. Then add some stripes.

6. Add big gloves and boots. Fill in with crayons.

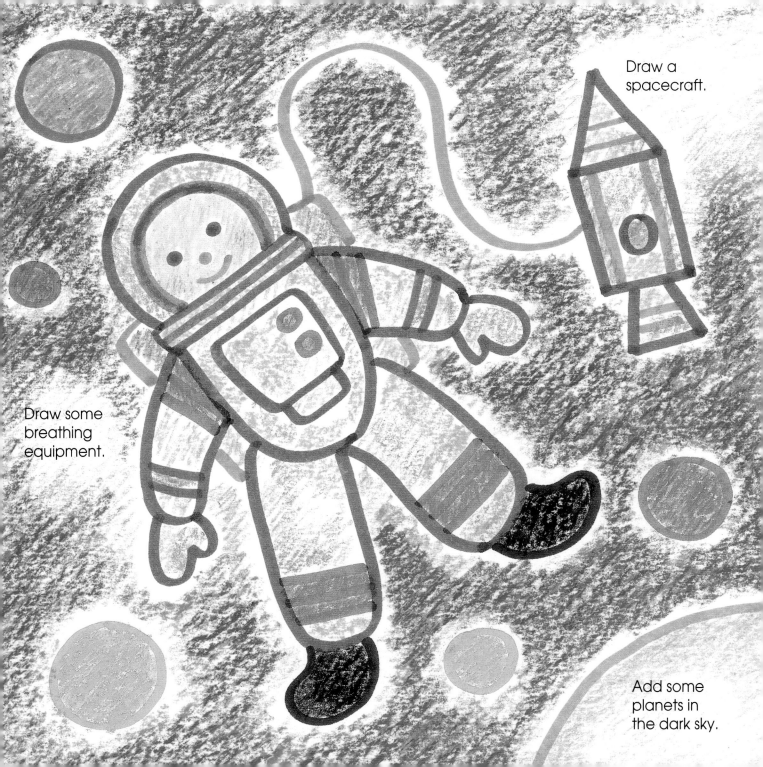

Draw a spacecraft.

Draw some breathing equipment.

Add some planets in the dark sky.

a parachutist

1. Use felt-tips for a head, crash helmet and goggles.

2. Draw a nose and mouth. Add the body.

3. Add the arms and hands.

4. Draw a harness and some straps.

Draw a parachute.

Add lines to the straps.

5. Draw the legs and feet.

6. Fill in with crayons.

20

Draw
the land
below.

a skier

You can't see the other leg.

1. Use a felt-tip to draw a head. Add a headband.

2. Draw the top part of the body and an arm.

3. Add a leg. Make it bend at the knee.

4. Draw a glove and a big, chunky ski boot.

5. Add a ski. Draw two ski poles, one going behind the body.

6. Add hair, some goggles and a mouth. Fill in with crayons.

Draw skiers on a slope far away.

Draw mountains and fir trees.

23

an ice skater

1. Use a felt-tip to draw her head and arms.

2. Draw the top part of her dress, below the arms.

3. Draw a short skirt and sleeves.

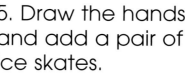

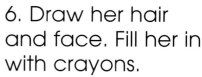

4. Add the legs. Make one of them bend at the knee.

5. Draw the hands and add a pair of ice skates.

6. Draw her hair and face. Fill her in with crayons.

Draw jewels
on her dress.

Add patches of
lights on the ice
and a yellow
spotlight.

a cowboy

1. Draw a hat with a felt-tip. Add the head.

2. Draw ears and the top of the body.

3. Draw the arms. Make one bend up, like this.

4. Draw a pair of jeans with a blue felt-tip.

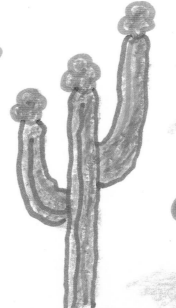

5. Add hands, a pair of boots and a jacket.

6. Add the face. Fill in the cowboy with crayons.

Give your cowboy a lasso.

Draw a scarf around the neck.

Draw some spurs on the boots.

faces

1. Draw a face with a felt-tip. Add the eyes.

2. Do a nose and a smiley mouth.

3. Draw the ears and eyebrows.

4. Fill in the face with a crayon.

Add wrinkles.

Add a hat.

Draw long hair.

Draw a bald head.

Add freckles.

Now try these

an angry
face

a sleeping
face

a surprised
face

a sad face

Draw
rosy cheeks.

Add
glasses.

Draw
curly
hair.

A sleeping
baby

Add earrings.

a horse and rider

1. Draw the horse's body with a felt-tip.

2. Draw a neck joined to the body.

3. Draw the head and an ear.

4. Draw four long legs. Add hooves.

5. Add the mane and a tail with a crayon.

6. Draw the rider's leg, like this.

Here are some different horses to draw.

Draw a horse eating grass.

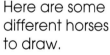

7. Do the body and a head.

8. Add a riding hat and a foot.

9. Add an arm and a hand.

10. Draw a nose band and reins.

11. Draw a face on the horse and rider.

12. Add some hair. Fill in with crayons.

Draw a horse pulling a cart.

Turn to the next page for a jumping horse.

Try drawing a
horse going
over a jump.

You could add
a saddle, too.